COOL CITIZENS

ROSIE McCORMICK

D0294401

Books

First published in the UK in 2002 by

Chrysalis Children's Books
An imprint of Chrysalis Books Group Plc
The Chrysalis Building, Bramley Road, London W10 6SP

Paperback edition first published in 2004

Editor: Kate Phelps
Designer: Peter Clayman
Illustrator: Woody
Consultant: Kathleen Robertson

ISBN 1 84138 428 3 (hb)
ISBN 1 84138 793 2 (pb)

British Library Cataloguing in Publication Data for this
book is available from the British Library.

Printed In China

Some of the more unfamiliar words used in this book
are explained in the glossary on pages 46 and 47.

CONTENTS

Dear Reader

Greetings citizen! You may never have thought of yourself as a 'citizen' but that's what you are. You are a citizen of the country you live in and indeed the whole planet.

What does that mean? Well, think about all the things you need to make your life run smoothly. They just seem to happen, don't they? Your meals are ready on time. You have a home, clothes, toys, furniture, water, electricity, a telephone, a tv, maybe a computer and a family car. You travel to school by bus or train. You learn useful things at school. Everything functions just fine without you having to give it too much thought!

But that's where you are wrong. You see, all of the things that make up a family, a community or a society rely completely on individuals just like you. Individuals who contribute their skills, knowledge and talents to each other – to you, to everyone. Each individual is an important part of a massive jigsaw. Each piece is essential. We are citizens working together to make sure our world is safe, happy, peaceful, fair and free.

INTRODUCTION

I bet you are wondering where you fit in. After all, you might think you are only a kid who goes to school, plays a lot, likes to eat loads and watch TV. But there are lots of things you can do, and probably already do. First of all you have a responsibility towards your family and friends, your school and your local community. By that I mean that you have a responsibility to behave in a thoughtful and caring way.

It's also important to understand how societies are organized and managed – especially if you are part of one – and you are. This book will help you discover some of the facts. And as a few of the pieces begin to fit, you will start to think about your place in the world.

Just remember one thing, we all live together on one planet. So our actions really do affect other people.

CITIZEN SPEAK
Your community is made up of the people who live near you.

A society is a large group of people who live in a place, such as a country.

ALL ABOUT CITIZENSHIP

Over hundreds of years people have discovered that it helps to have a number of rules and regulations in place to keep our world in order. We've learnt this the hard way. Here are a couple of examples.

RUBBISH RULES

It used to be that you could throw your rubbish out on to the roads and streets outside your home. There were no rules to stop anyone from doing this. This proved to be dirty, smelly and unhygienic. People died from all kinds of diseases. So eventually laws were passed to stop this happening. People's rubbish was collected instead and taken away.

'pewhee!'

CAR CHAOS

When people first started driving cars, there weren't any rules about how to behave on the road. So people just did whatever they wanted to. As more and more people took to the roads in their cars, it soon became clear that some rules wouldn't go amiss.

Ruth walked all the way home from school every day. After a while her teacher asked her – 'Ruth why don't you take the bus sometimes?'
Ruth: I can't, I'm not allowed to take anything that doesn't belong to me!

'Let's go backwards!'

So if there's a rule or a law, there's usually a good reason for it.

At Home

Usually the first rules you come across are the ones your mum, dad and various other adults impose on you. Sometimes they can seem unfair and boring. But without them life at home could become a little chaotic!

These guidelines are really intended to keep you safe and teach you how to behave, not just at home but in the great, big, wide world.

COOL RULES FOR COOL CITIZENS

1. Listen to what your mum or dad has to say
2. Be thoughtful towards your brothers and sisters
3. Always say 'please' and 'thank you'
4. Look after your belongings
5. Be helpful, considerate and kind

DON'T DROP A CLASSROOM CLANGER

1. Be kind and offer to help
2. Put your hand up before speaking
3. Don't run in the classroom
4. Do the best work that you can
5. Let others have their say

At School

As soon as you start school you discover that there are even more rules to follow in order to stay out of trouble. But if you think about them carefully, they are there to make sure you enjoy school as much as possible.

RUNNING THE COUNTRY

Now, it can be difficult managing just one family or school even when everyone does what's expected of them. So imagine what it must be like managing and organizing whole communities, not to mention countries. This is what governments do. To help them manage fairly there are rules, called laws, to remind everyone how to behave. People involved in both local and national government are responsible for making the most of these rules and regulations. They are also responsible for making sure that every aspect of our society works the way it should. This is how it's all done:

NATIONAL GOVERNMENT

The United Kingdom has a political system in which people can vote representatives into government. This is known as a democracy. The Parliament is where the representatives (the Members of Parliament) meet to discuss ideas and make laws. It is made up of the House of Commons, the House of Lords and the Head of State. The House of Commons is known as the lower chamber (division) of Parliament and is where the Members of Parliament meet. The House of Lords is the upper chamber and is made up of peers of the realm (lords and ladies). The Head of State is Queen Elizabeth II.

GOVERNMENT BODIES

The government is made up of three parts:
• the legislature (the part which makes and passes laws)
• the executive (the part which runs the country)
• the judiciary (the courts, which make decisions about how laws are enforced)

LOCAL AFFAIRS

As well as this, Wales and Northern Ireland have their own governing bodies, called assemblies, made up of elected members who concentrate on local concerns. And Scotland has a Scottish government concerned with Scottish affairs.

THE GOVERNMENT

A government is chosen during a general election. People vote and the party that gets the largest number of Members of Parliament (MPs) elected to the House of Commons forms the new government.
The government is led by a newly appointed Prime Minister, Deputy Prime Minister and about 100 specially selected members.

'Yippee, I've won!'

Closed for holidays!

SITTING HOUSE

A Parliament can sit (meet) for a maximum of five years, usually divided into one-year sessions. As Head of State, the Queen makes a speech to Parliament at the beginning of each session. The Queen's Speech outlines the government's policies for that year. In other words, it explains what the government plans to do. Parliament is officially closed just in time for the summer holidays.

THE CABINET

The Cabinet is a group of about 20 ministers especially chosen by the Prime Minister to help him or her govern. The Cabinet has a great deal of responsibility as its members are in charge of deciding what the government will do.

GOVERNMENT DEPARTMENTS

Special departments and agencies help the government to carry out its policies. The staff, called civil servants, carry out the work. They report to ministers who then inform Parliament of their progress. Some (but not all) government departments are known by their initials. See if you can work out which of these goes with which department: DFES, DEFRA, DTLR, DH, MoD, DCMS, DTI.

Some government departments are:
• Department for Environment, Food and Rural Affairs
• Department of Culture, Media and Sport
• Ministry of Defence
• Department for Education and Skills
• Department of Transport, Local Government and the Regions
• Department of Health
• Home Office
• Department of Trade and Industry
• HM Treasury

THE CIVIL SERVICE

Civil servants advise ministers and work on government policies. Their job is to work for the good of the current government. They do not favour a political party.

THE HOUSES OF PARLIAMENT

The main functions of Parliament are:
- to pass laws
- to vote for the taxes (money people pay to the government) and expenditure that enable the government to carry out its work
- to look closely at how the government is working
- to discuss important issues

LOCAL GOVERNMENT

Who do you think is responsible for keeping your roads clean and safe, collecting your rubbish, making sure local transport runs on time and that your school provides you with a good education? Well it's the job of local authorities, or councils, to do this. Some councils look after more than one million people, others are responsible for just a few thousand.

11

HUMAN RIGHTS

It may interest you to know that the country you live in has made sure that your best interests, well being and safety are protected. On 2 October 2000 the Human Rights Act became law. That meant that for the first time, citizens of the United Kingdom have a number of clearly stated rights that protect them from unfair treatment. We are lucky because not every country in the world provides such protection for its citizens.

What's the difference between a burglar and a church bell? One steals from the people and one peels for the people.

I love carrots and think they should be free!

Your rights as a citizen of the United Kingdom include:
- the right to life
- a ban on torture
- a ban on slavery
- the right to liberty
- the right to a fair trial
- freedom of thought and religion
- freedom of expression
- the right to marry and have a family
- the right to education

All kinds of people

A country is not just made up of governments. Most importantly, it is made up of a rich variety of different kinds of people. And although there are laws guiding our behaviour, we are still able to be different and individual.

Different but alike

Take a look around you. Your friends are all physically different. Some are taller, shorter, have different colour eyes, hair and skin. They or their parents may come originally from different countries and they may be able to speak different languages. These are differences that make life richer and more interesting. But in just as many ways we are the same. We want to be safe, happy and free to live life to the full.

A good citizen

We have a responsibility to care for each other's well being. It is not acceptable to be mean to someone because you think they are different from you. Just imagine yourself in a foreign place. You would be considered a little different too. Then imagine how frightened you would feel if people didn't want to talk to you or play with you or, even worse, wanted to harm you. So remember, your job as a citizen is to help build a peaceful world. Maybe you could start in the playground!

FOOTBALL TODAY 12.30 EVERYONE WELCOME

13

RACE ISSUES

Some people believe that the human race can be divided into different races or groups. Often these races are based on colour of skin. In the United Kingdom, it is illegal to treat someone differently because of their race. It is against the law to stir up racial hatred.

EQUALITY OF THE SEXES

Laws in this country ensure that men and women are treated equally. It is illegal to pay men and women different amounts of money for the same kind of work. It is illegal to discriminate (treat differently) between men and women in relation to education. It is illegal to treat men and women differently at work in terms of job opportunities, promotion, transfers and training.

'Morning!'

THE LAW AND DISABILITY

Disabled people have a right not to be discriminated against at work or when they're trying to find a job. This means they must be treated as the equals of people without disabilities.

14

BELIEFS

Because of our history, the United Kingdom has a great variety of religions. And we are all free to practise our own particular religious beliefs.

The six largest religious groups are:
- Christians
- Muslims
- Hindus
- Sikhs
- Jews
- Buddhists

CHRISTIANS

Members of the Christian Church worship God through Jesus. They believe that God sent his son to us in the form of Jesus to guide us and bring us closer to God. The celebrations, or holy days, of the Christian Church are mostly to do with the life of Jesus and the Christian saints.

MUSLIMS

The five requirements of Islam are: to worship one God, Allah; to pray five times a day; to help the poor; to fast; and to go to Mecca, a place of pilgrimage, once in a person's lifetime. Islamic festivals celebrate the Prophet Muhammad and other prophets.

HINDUS

Hinduism is based on the practice of Dharma, the code of life. Unlike other religions, Hinduism does not have a single founder or a single belief. At the centre of Hinduism are Brahma the Creator, Vishnu the preserver and Shiva the Destroyer.

SIKHS

The Sikhs, or disciples, are followers of Guru Nanak and nine other gurus. The goal of Sikhs is to build a close relationship with God. They believe in one all powerful God, but their God can have many names and can be worshipped in many different ways.

16

JEWS

Judaism is an ancient religion and was the first one to have at its centre a single God. It is based on trust in God and the desire to carry out his wishes as laid down in the Ten Commandments.

BUDDHISTS

Buddhists follow the teachings of the Lord Buddha, the founder of their faith. With his words as guidance Buddhists strive to achieve a high level of spirituality.

WORLD CITIZENS

As well as understanding how our own society works, it's also important to remember that we belong to an even bigger world. A world that is made up of different kinds of people, cultures and governments. And although we may be separated by oceans and continents, languages and beliefs, we all share one common experience. We live together on this planet – Earth. This fact alone brings us together and makes us all responsible for the wellbeing of our world.

GLOBAL VILLAGE

The world's population is getting bigger. There are over 6 billion of us on this planet. Yet modern ways of communicating, such as telephones and e-mail, and fast forms of transport, such as jet planes, have made it easier than ever to stay in touch with people around the world. This is what people mean when they say we live in a 'global village'.

www...com

No country can isolate itself from the rest of the world. The United Kingdom is a member of many international bodies including the **European Union** (made up of many European countries) and the **North Atlantic Treaty Organization** (or NATO, an alliance between the United States of America and many European countries). Perhaps one day there will be a world government. What do you think its mission might be?

Respect the Earth

Because our planet provides us with so much – air, water, food, shelter, life itself – we most certainly have a responsibility to look after it and protect it from harm. Global pollution and the destruction of rainforests and wildlife are very serious problems. Fortunately, all over the world, children just like you are speaking up for Planet Earth and helping out by recycling waste, cleaning up polluted areas and protecting the natural world. And wherever there is poverty, disease, war and distress people just like you raise money and send aid.

So it seems that if the citizens of Planet Earth continue to work together and help each other, our future is undoubtedly bright and hopeful, especially if we follow these guidelines.

COOL RULES FOR COOL WORLD CITIZENS
1. Respect all people
2. Be tolerant
3. Be proud of your family, race and culture
4. Strive to do good things
5. Protect and care for the environment

Quiz Time

Now just to make sure that you've been paying attention here's a little quiz to test your memory.

1 Who is in charge of the government?
a) The Prime Minister
b) The Queen
c) A civil servant

2 Who is the Head of State?
a) The Queen
b) The Prime Minister
c) The headmaster

3 What is the maximum length of time that a Parliament can sit for?
a) 3 years
b) 5 years
c) 10 years

4 How many ministers make up the Cabinet?
a) 10 ministers
b) 30 ministers
c) 20 ministers

5 What makes up the United Kingdom's Parliament?
a) The House of Commons, the House of Lords and the Head of State
b) Just the House of Commons
c) The House of Commons and the House of Lords

6 What is the United Kingdom's general code of rights called?
a) The Citizens' Rights Act
b) The Human Rights Act
c) The People's Rights Act

7 Who is in charge of keeping roads safe and clean and of collecting rubbish?
a) Parliament
b) The Cabinet
c) Local government

8 Which of these is illegal?
a) To discriminate against people because of their race
b) To pay men and women different amounts for the same work
c) To treat someone differently because they are disabled

9 What is Mecca?
a) A Muslim place of pilgrimage
b) A Sikh place of pilgrimage
c) A Christian place of pilgrimage

10 Which religion was the first to have a single God?
a) The Jewish faith
b) The Christian faith
c) The Buddhist faith

11 How many people live on this planet?
a) 1 million
b) 6 million
c) 6 billion

12 Which of these is an international body?
a) United Kingdom
b) European Union
c) United States of America

ANSWERS

21

They're only words

'Hurry up James, you're going to be late,' called James' mum from the kitchen. 'Come downstairs and eat your breakfast now please. And don't forget to bring your homework with you!'

James ignored his mum. Instead he got up from the bedroom floor, where he had been sitting, and lay down on his unmade bed. He was kind of dressed for school. He had put on his shirt, trousers, socks and shoes. But his blazer and tie still lay draped across a chair. James' school books lay open on his desk, his homework unfinished.

IT'S A FACT
Discrimination is any kind of treatment or action that favours one person or group over another.

James didn't like going to school. In fact he absolutely hated it. Not because he didn't like learning new things or because he disliked his teacher. No. The simple truth was that James was afraid to go to school.

James heard his mother's footsteps on the stairs and jumped up from his bed. He scrambled to his desk and quickly crammed his books and his unfinished homework into his school bag. Then grabbing his jacket and tie he made it out of his bedroom and on to the landing just in time to prevent another outburst from his mum.

'Thank goodness. I was beginning to think I was talking to myself,' said James' mother with a smile. 'You have 15 minutes to eat your breakfast, now hurry up.' And with that James' mum began to storm her way through his bedroom, picking up dirty clothes and muttering as she went.

James sat down at the kitchen table and poured himself some cereal. But he could only manage one mouthful. His stomach was doing somersaults and food made him feel physically sick. More than anything James was angry with himself for feeling so scared.

Upstairs his mum was humming as she tidied up the bedrooms. Then, when she had finished, James heard her go into the bathroom to put her make-up on for work. James sat at the kitchen table listening to her cheerfully shuffle around. Less than one month ago they had moved from London to a small market town. James had started a new school and his mum had started a new job. His mum seemed so much happier. It was as if she thought that life's complicated jigsaw pieces had finally slotted into place. There was no way he could tell her about what was happening to him at his new school, Orchard Primary. Somehow he had to try to deal with the problem himself.

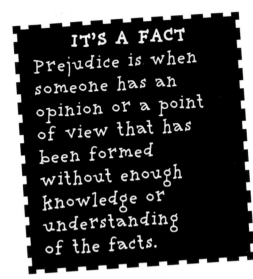

IT'S A FACT
Prejudice is when someone has an opinion or a point of view that has been formed without enough knowledge or understanding of the facts.

Twenty minutes later, James was waving to his mother as she drove away from the school gates. He waited until her car was completely out of sight before turning and walking into school. His legs felt like heavy lead weights as he crossed the playground towards the spot where his class would soon be lining up to go inside. James kept his eyes down, not daring to look at anyone, just in case they were there.

And they were.

24

'Hey! I thought I told you that me and my friends didn't want to see your black face in this school any more. So how come you're still here? What's the problem, don't you understand English black boy?!'

And with that, James was pushed backwards, forwards and then on to the ground by the group of four boys who had surrounded him. Their ringleader was a fifth-year boy called David Thomson. He always started the trouble.

Just then the bell rang. James struggled to his feet as the gang of four moved like lightning and hid themselves in the swarm of school children moving across the playground. James dusted himself down, picked up his school bag and made his way to the back of his fourth-year line.

'James, what on earth have you done to your head?' said his teacher, Miss Houghton, as James filed passed her.

'Er, I tripped in the playground,' replied James without looking up.

IT'S A FACT
Discriminating against people because of their race, colour, nationality, ethnic or national origin has been illegal in England, Wales and Scotland since 1976, and in Northern Ireland since 1997.

25

'Well you'd better run along to Mrs Wilson and ask her to clean that up. You're going to need a plaster as well.'

Mrs Wilson was the school secretary but she was also trained in first aid. She was just about to sit down to her first cup of tea of the day when James knocked on her office door. Mrs Wilson looked up to see James standing in the open doorway with a nasty graze on his forehead.

26

'Oh James what ever have you done now?' asked Mrs Wilson.

'I tripped,' replied James quietly.

'What, again? Honestly James, you really have to be more careful,' said Mrs Wilson between 'tutting' sounds. Then she bathed the cut on his head and covered it with a large, square plaster.

James returned to his classroom where his teacher was just about to start a history lesson. She smiled at James as he walked towards his desk. History was his favourite subject. He particularly liked this term's topic, the Romans in Britain. But he could not concentrate on anything Miss Houghton was saying. All he could think about was what was going to happen to him at playtime.

All through the lesson, James kept his head down and tried not to attract Miss Houghton's attention. He hardly heard a word she said. He breathed as quietly as he could. He did not stir. James simply wanted to be invisible.

This was so different from how things had been at his old school in London. There he would have had millions of things to say about Roman Britain and the life of a legionnaire. It was also different because James was just one of many children whose parents, grandparents or even the children themselves came from different parts of the world. No one seemed to notice or even care that he was black.

When the bell rang for break time, Miss Houghton instructed the children to put their books away and to form an orderly line in front of the door. The other children were happy and eager to get outside to play. But James moved slowly, reluctantly, trying to hold back the moment when he would have to leave the safety of the classroom.

James stepped outside and felt the warm spring air on his face. All around him children were running, skipping and having fun. In the corner of the playground some of the boys from his class were kicking a football around. Jason waved at him to come and join in.

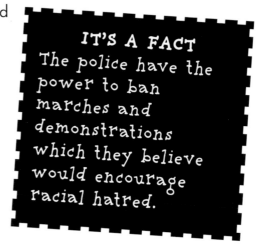

IT'S A FACT
The police have the power to ban marches and demonstrations which they believe would encourage racial hatred.

But James simply shook his head. Instead he stood alone not far from the main door, willing the 15 minutes of playtime to be over.

'Hey black boy, what do you think you're looking at?' said a horribly familiar voice. 'How'd you get that bump on your head...fall out of a banana tree?'

Then James felt a hand on his shoulder and he lurched forward. He turned around to see David Thomson's sneering face. As usual he had his gang with him.

'Look, just leave me alone,' said James. 'I'm not bothering you am I?'

'Oh but that's where you're wrong black boy. You see your black face really does bother me. You shouldn't be here,' continued David, his face twisted and angry.

'Oh really! Where should I be then?' snapped James as he struggled not to let his temper get the better of him.

'You should be in your own country, sunshine!' replied David as he shoved James backwards.

James managed to correct his balance and stop himself from falling.

'Well for your information I was born in Britain, in London actually, so this is my country!' shouted James. He was angry and upset. He couldn't recall a moment in his life when he had felt so enraged. He clenched his fists tightly and willed himself not to lash out and hit David Thomson.

'You think you're smart do yer?' said David between gritted teeth. 'We'll show you how smart you are. Come on guys...' and with that David and his gang began shoving James around. Unable to keep his balance, James fell backwards, hitting his head against a small ornamental wall.

James opened his eyes to see Mrs Wilson and Miss Houghton staring back at him. His head was pounding and he struggled to remember exactly what had happened.

'Oh James, James can you hear me?' cried an emotional Mrs Wilson. She was kneeling beside him and stroking his head. 'You've been unconscious for a few minutes. You were knocked out when you hit the wall. An ambulance is coming to take you to hospital. My goodness James, how long has this been going on?'

James was silent. He couldn't bring himself to talk about the events of the previous few weeks. He had never encountered racism before. It had made him feel numb and empty inside. It had made him feel like an outsider. All he could do was stare at Mrs Wilson's white hand as she rested it gently on his shoulder.

'James I saw what happened,' Miss Houghton interjected. 'And from what some of the other children have told me, this is not the first time you've been injured. I'm so sorry that you didn't think you could tell me.'

'I wanted to sort it out myself,' whispered James. 'It's my problem.'

'No James, it's not your problem. It's David Thomson's problem. And the others who joined in,' continued Miss Houghton. 'They are all in very serious trouble. There will be an investigation and if what we suspect is true, there will be severe disciplinary action. Now we've phoned your mum, and Mrs Wilson is going with you to the local hospital. Your mum will meet you there.'

32

'You've told my mum,' sighed James.
'I didn't want her to know anything about this. It will spoil everything for her.'

Several hours later James was home from the hospital and tucked up in bed. He was suffering from a bad headache and a nasty bump. But the worst feeling of all was the one he had inside. He felt like he didn't belong anymore. Worst of all, he felt that somehow he had let his mum down. Just then his bedroom door opened and his mum came in carrying a tray laden with goodies. There were burger and chips, a fizzy drink and an enormous bowl of ice cream. James' mum sat down on the edge of his bed and rubbed his head.

'I hope you are hungry,' she said with a smile.

James sat up and took the tray from her but he did not say anything. Then slowly, silently he began to eat.

His mum watched him for a while and then she said, 'James, I'm very proud of you. You are a strong and brave boy,' she said.

'Oh no I'm not. I just stood there and took it. I should have fought back,' said James angrily. 'I'm bigger than David Thomson. I could have really hurt him if I'd wanted to. If it had just been me and him. But he always brought his friends along so that they could have a go as well!'

'James the best way to stop people like David Thomson and his friends is to speak up... speak out. All forms of abuse thrive when there is silence. The sad truth is there are people in the world that do think like David Thomson does. They are ignorant and afraid of things they don't understand or things that are different. They lash out and cause a great deal of misery and pain. Unfortunately I can't protect you from this. I just wish you had told me about what was happening to you,' said his mum sadly.

'They don't like me just because I'm black,' said James bitterly.

'James I suspect that David Thomson and the others don't fully understand what they are saying. They're still children. They've heard others, probably adults, saying bad things. They do the same just to act big. It doesn't excuse for one moment what they have done to you. And one thing's for sure, they are going to be punished. But you mustn't lose sight of the fact that you are my beautiful boy. We are black and we are very proud of our heritage. The colour of a person's skin can tell others a little bit about who they are, but only in relation to where in the world they or their ancestors come from. The truth is these boys don't know you. They haven't even tried to get to know you,' continued James' mum.

34

'The things they said were worse than what they did,' sighed James. 'They're only words but they can really hurt.'

'Words are very powerful weapons. Words can make good and bad things happen. That is why it is so important to speak up; to say something,' said James' mum.

'Do I have to go back to school?' asked James with a worried look on his face.

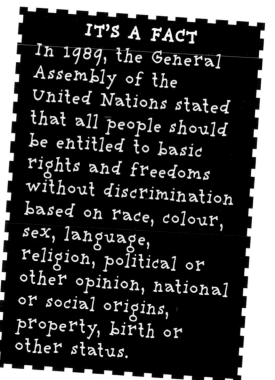

IT'S A FACT

In 1989, the General Assembly of the United Nations stated that all people should be entitled to basic rights and freedoms without discrimination based on race, colour, sex, language, religion, political or other opinion, national or social origins, property, birth or other status.

James' mum looked at him for a few moments without answering. Then she said, 'James, when I first heard about what those boys had done to you, I wanted to scream. Then I wanted to confront them – and their parents. But since then I've had several conversations with your Head Teacher. Mrs Lewis has promised me – us – that David Thomson and the others will be excluded from school. In other words there will be an investigation. And with so many of your class mates willing to talk about how you were bullied, and the fact that Miss Houghton saw them push you around, it seems certain that they won't be around to bother you again. So, if you would like to give things another try, then I will as well. But I want it to be your decision James,' replied his mum.

James did not answer.

'By the way, while you were taking a nap, a boy called Jason dropped this off for you,' said James' mum as she handed him an envelope.

James opened the envelope to find a card with a picture of a golden lion wearing a red crown. The card read:

Jason xxx

Dear James,

We are so sorry for what happened to you. Please come back to school soon. We all want to be your friend.

Love from Class Four

The card was full of names followed by kisses and drawings of flowers, cars and stars. Next to Jason's name was a picture of two boys playing football. Jason had written his name and James' name underneath his stick figures.

James put the card on his bedside table and looked at his mum. 'Maybe it's worth trying again,' said James quietly. 'Mum, perhaps I could invite Jason round to play. What do you think?'

'I think that's a great idea,' said James' mum with a smile. 'Now eat the rest of your tea while I tidy up this mess.'

James watched his mum as she attempted to tidy up his room again. For the first time in ages he felt like his old self. The feelings of loneliness and fear had gone. Now it seemed like there really were things to look forward to.

CITIZEN SUPERSTARS

Two particularly clever men helped to develop the idea of society and citizenship. And although they didn't agree with each other about these issues, they both had some interesting things to say. But first here's some background...

FIRST CITIZENS

The very idea that people could become citizens of a place probably began in Athens, Greece, thousands of years ago. Then, in this ancient city-state, citizenship was granted to mostly upper-class males. Over time, certain foreigners and freed slaves were also allowed to become citizens. Citizenship was also important to the people of ancient Rome. Citizens were responsible for running the government of Rome. A Roman boy became a citizen at 16 or 17 years of age. This was a very important occasion and the boy's family held celebrations to honour a new citizen of Rome.

PLATO

428–347 BC

Plato was a brilliant teacher and philosopher. He founded a school called the Academy. It became the most famous school in the ancient world, and Aristotle its most famous pupil. Plato had an interesting way of teaching. He wrote down imaginary conversations between

himself and his former teacher Socrates. Then he used these imaginary chats in his school as starting points for lessons or discussions. The most famous of these discussions is called *The Republic* and in it Plato asks questions like – 'what is a just and good individual?' He also debated how citizens should be educated, what kinds of governments work best and who should be allowed to govern.

ARISTOTLE
384–322 BC

Aristotle was an ancient Greek philosopher and scientist. Along with his teacher, Plato, he is thought to be one of the most influential people who ever lived. Aristotle believed that just because you were born in a place, this did not make you a citizen. And he did not believe that all people were equal. Instead, Aristotle said that citizenship is for those who have the ability to govern others. Just think, if this were how things were done today, only those in government would be able to call themselves citizens!

★ SIGN HERE

Long ago, kings and queens were very bossy and tended to get their own way. This changed somewhat when, in 1215, angry lords made King John of England sign a Great Charter, known as the Magna Carta. This Charter stated that people could not be imprisoned without trial, that citizens could own and inherit property and new taxes had to be approved by the Great Council, or Parliament.

★ DON'T LOSE YOUR HEAD

Disagreements about how best to govern have gone on for hundreds of years and still go on today. Sometimes the disagreements can be quite serious. In 1649, Parliament and the King of England fell out in a big way over who should have the most power. The king, Charles I, lost and was executed (his head was cut off) in the same year.

Where was the Magna Carta signed? **At the bottom.**

★ NO PAINE, NO GAIN

Up until the eighteenth century, the government of most countries was in the hands of a few people. In 1791, a man called Thomas Paine wrote a book called *The Rights of Man*. In it he suggested that all people had a right to be involved in government, not just a privileged few. His book was published in many countries and encouraged people to demand change.

★ SPOIL SPORT

The famous philosopher Plato believed in banning pieces of music, art and literature if they did not encourage good behaviour and set a good example. In fact if Plato were alive today, he would certainly want to prevent children from watching tv, listening to most popular music or reading comic books!

★ LONG SERVICE

If you were a member of the Roman army, you became a citizen of ancient Rome. But there was a high price to pay for this privilege. You had to serve in the army for 25 years.

★ PEOPLE POWER

Many governments are based on the principles of democracy, which means that all citizens have the right to vote for their government. The word democracy comes from the Greek words *demos*, meaning 'people', and *krakos*, meaning 'power'.

★ OUT LOUD

Long ago, when most people couldn't read, people received most of their news and information from town criers. They stood in a public square and shouted out important pieces of news and explained new laws and taxes.

'By the King's command there is to be a new tax on warts. If you have any, you have to pay a fine!'

★ WASTEFUL

Each year in the UK, we throw away almost 30 million tonnes of household waste. Most of this ends up in the ground in what are called landfill sites. Gases from the waste pollute the air and the decaying waste can pollute underground rivers.

Teacher: 'Who can tell me when Rome was built?'
Brian: 'During the night'.
Teacher: 'Why do you say that?'
Brian: 'Because my mum says that Rome wasn't built in a day'.

★ CAR JAM

There are more than 550 million vehicles in the world with more being produced each day. If they all formed an orderly queue, they would stretch round the world four times!

THINGS TO DO

1 With your family or classmates, create a code of conduct that you would like people to honour either at home or at school.

2 Imagine that you are running for local election. Write a speech and design a poster for your campaign. In your speech, outline all the things you would like to do for your community.

3 When you go to the countryside you will discover that, even in such wide open spaces, you have a responsibility to pay attention to what's happening around you. Learn the countryside rules and encourage others to do so as well.

Rules of the countryside
- Guard against risk of fire
- Take special care on country roads
- Leave farm animals, crops and machinery alone
- Fasten all gates
- Keep your dog under control
- Take your litter home
- Make no unnecessary noise
- Protect wildlife, plants and trees

4 With your class and teacher, invite a member of your local council responsible for waste disposal to visit your school. Before the visit try to find out as much as you can about the main types of waste in your area. Ask the council member how and where waste is disposed of – especially harmful waste products.

5 Set up a school council and elect members who will present pupils' issues and concerns to teachers.

6 Imagine that you were in charge of the whole world for just one day. What things would you do to make it a better place?

USEFUL INFORMATION

Here are some web sites that contain useful information about citizenship. The Internet is constantly changing so if you can't find some of these web sites, you can use any search engine to find what you are looking for. Try words like 'citizenship' and 'government'.

Information and projects to do with waste disposal: www.schools-citizenship.com

Global express offers a teacher's resource for classroom discussions on citizenship and current news events: www.dep.org.uk/globalexpress

A useful site that discusses all aspects of citizenship: www.citizensconnection.net

The site of the Citizenship Foundation: www.citfou.org.uk

The charity Save the Children's web site: www.savethechildren.org.uk

Children can exchange ideas on citizenship on this site: www.timeforcitizenship.com

The site of the Prime Minister: www.pm.gov.uk

The web site of the charity, Oxfam: www.oxfam.org

GLOSSARY

CITIZEN A person who by birth or by choice is a member of a nation.

COMMUNITY People that live in the same place or area.

CONTINENT One of the seven large land masses on Earth.

COUNCIL A group of people who meet to discuss issues and give advice.

CULTURE The traditions, customs, language, arts and so on of a particular group of people or nation.

DEMOCRACY A nation that is governed by the people or their elected representatives.

DISABILITY A physical or mental condition that can sometimes prevent someone from doing a particular thing.

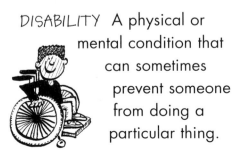

DISCRIMINATION To treat someone unfairly because of race, religion, culture, disability or other such reasons.

ENVIRONMENT Surroundings in which people, animals and plants live.

EQUALITY To be equal or treated the same as everyone else.

FESTIVAL A celebration often linked to a religious event or historical occurrence.

GENERAL ELECTION A time when all representatives stand for election in order to become members of the government.

GLOBAL Something that relates to the whole world.

GOVERNMENT The means of ruling a country, county, city or other such place.

INTERNATIONAL Something that involves other nations.

LAW A specific rule which people are required to follow.

NATIONAL Something that relates or is connected to a nation as a whole.

PARLIAMENT An assembly of elected representatives who meet to govern, pass laws and discuss issues.

POLICY A plan or guideline that explains how something works.

POVERTY To be without the most basic human requirements such as enough food to eat and adequate shelter and clothing.

PREJUDICE To form an opinion based on ignorance of all the facts.

RACE The division of all human beings into particular groups often defined by physical characteristics.

RELIGION A particular divine belief.

RESPONSIBILITY To be responsible for a particular thing.

SOCIETY People living together as a group.

TAX Money paid by people to the government; this money is used to fund hospitals, schools, public transport and so on.

VOTE The means of choosing a government representative.

WORSHIP To pray or honour God.

INDEX